Original title:
Finding Purpose in the Weirdest Places

Copyright © 2025 Creative Arts Management OÜ
All rights reserved.

Author: Gideon Shaw
ISBN HARDBACK: 978-1-80566-201-3
ISBN PAPERBACK: 978-1-80566-496-3

The Muse of Mismatched Furniture

In a chair that wobbles like a dance,
An old lamp flickers, taking its chance.
The table's leg is short, oh dear!
But somehow, magic lingers here.

A couch with colors that clash and fight,
An armrest that offers no respite.
Yet laughter echoes off the walls,
In this odd ensemble, joy enthralls.

Journeys in a Sock Drawer

A sock with stripes and one that's plain,
They travel together, though none complain.
They slip and slide in a cozy heap,
Dreaming of adventures, oh so deep.

A missing partner from a different pair,
Found in a corner, without a care.
Together they plot some wacky scheme,
To escape the drawer and chase a dream.

The Serendipity of Strangely Shaped Clouds

Look! A dolphin in a fluff of white,
A pickle-shaped wonder, what a sight!
They twist and turn in the open sky,
Tickling our minds as they drift by.

Some say they're dragons, others just fluff,
But their bizarre shapes are always enough.
They giggle and dance in the sun's embrace,
Bringing laughter to our curious chase.

The Beauty of Abandoned Dreams

In a drawer, a sketch of a grand guitar,
Collecting dust, but still a star.
The pages rustle with whispers bold,
Of melodies waiting to be told.

A dream to surf on the moon's bright face,
Left behind, but still holds grace.
In shadows, they wait for a silly push,
To jump back into life, with a joyful whoosh.

Secrets Beneath the Swing Set

The swing set creaks in the breeze,
Hiding secrets, just like trees.
A cat in shades, sunbathing there,
Contemplating life without a care.

Chalk drawings dance on the ground,
Telling tales that won't make a sound.
The slide whispers of laughter and fun,
Where dreams of escape are spun and run.

Forgotten toys buried in sand,
Guard mysteries no one had planned.
A rubber duck with an enigmatic grin,
Could this be where the joy begins?

As we swing, we float and soar,
Reaching heights never reached before.
Perhaps the truth lies in a giggle,
Or a silly dance that makes us wiggle.

The Art of Finding Light in Shadows

In corners where dust bunnies frolic,
Shadows thick as a comic's knoll.
A blink reveals the silliness,
Of hidden hopes and giggles roll.

Underneath a sunbeam's glimmer,
Old socks perform a tango dance.
Sticky note reminders flicker,
Of random joys that dare to prance.

The coffee mug sings a tune,
While chairs gossip about the moon.
Socks that mismatched waltz away,
An art that brightens mundane gray.

Behind the curtains, secrets stir,
Crafting smiles in a little blur.
Among the odd, the strange, and bright,
We find our way back to delight.

Epiphany by the Old Train Tracks

The rusty tracks tell tales in time,
Of trains that danced and crossed a crime.
A pigeon in a top hat sits,
As if to judge our little wits.

A lost glove waves like a flag,
While memories makes our hearts lag.
We giggle at the passing breeze,
That teases like a childhood tease.

A ticket stub sings 'Adventure awaits!'
Whispers of far-off fateful dates.
The clatter of past passengers' feet,
Turns the mundane into a treat.

With every step, we stumble and lure,
Finding mischief where tracks demure.
Train whistles echo in the distance,
A reminder to embrace persistence.

The Unseen Theater of the Everyday

In the kitchen, spoons take a bow,
Quirky pots perform, 'What's that now?'
Coffee beans chatter in their grind,
Cooking up dreams that tease the mind.

The clock ticks wildly, a jester's show,
'Time's a trickster!' it seems to crow.
As dust motes dance in the sunbeam,
Life's absurdity makes us beam.

The cat curls up, steals the scene,
A liquid puddle in shades of green.
The fridge hums a lullaby,
As left-over pizza dreams to fly.

With every spatula's swish and swash,
We find ourselves in a playful quash.
The ordinary unfolds with grace,
In this unseen, delightful place.

Revelations in the Hall of Forgotten Toys

In corners where old toys conspire,
With dust bunnies and dreams that expire.
A rubber duck quacks tales so grand,
Of pirate ships and a forgotten land.

The dolls wink with secrets untold,
As stories of yore in their crannies unfold.
A teddy bear grumbles, 'I'm still the best!'
While action figures flex in their quest.

Marbles roll with echoes of cheer,
That summon laughter year after year.
Yet each piece is odd, a bit out of place,
A riot of quirks in this toy-filled space.

So let's raise a toast to the memories made,
In this whimsical hall, where time's gently swayed.
For here in the chaos, you'll truly see,
That purpose can sprout where you least expect to be.

The Wisdom of an Unraveled Sweater

An old sweater, once snug and neat,
Now sprawls like a cat with two left feet.
With holes like secrets, it tells a tale,
Of a home where warmth might sometimes fail.

Threads dangle like thoughts, a wild display,
Whispers of laughter from yesterday.
While sleeves flop about with a comical grace,
Knitting adventures in an unkempt space.

Each stitch tells a story, of tea spills and dreams,
Of cozy nights curled up by moonbeams.
But how can such chaos, a fashion faux pas,
Hold wisdom of life, like a quirky mantra?

So here's to the sweater, unraveling wide,
A testament to comfort, it wears with pride.
It shows us we're meant to embrace every flaw,
For the weirdest places can hold the most awe.

Secrets Beneath the Floorboards

Beneath the floor, where shadows loom,
Lies a treasure trove that smiles through gloom.
Old socks and crumbs from long-lost meals,
Bear witness to laughter and clattering heels.

A rogue toy soldier stands on guard,
With tales of battles fought and marred.
Though dusty and dim in this secret space,
Each relic is rich, full of odd grace.

Haunting whispers dance with creaks at night,
As memories play, bringing sheer delight.
For a lonely floorboard may seem absurd,
Yet echoes of joy cannot be unheard.

So let's lift the floor, peer into the deep,
Where secrets lie hidden, not meant for sleep.
For in the strangest nooks and oddest sights,
We might just find laughter in peculiar bites.

Illuminations from a Dusty Attic

In the attic atop the world's highest loft,
Shadows dance playfully, spinning quite soft.
A chandelier of cobwebs sways in the breeze,
While old trunks whisper like graphite leaves.

Here lies a hat that once held a dream,
Of a dapper fellow who danced in a theme.
With feathers askew, it tells tales anew,
Of parties that sparked under skies deep blue.

A trunk stuffed with letters, all yellowed and torn,
Whispers of love in the break of dawn.
And forgotten lampshades, with a curious glaze,
Illuminate laughter through completely odd ways.

So embrace the oddities, the dust and the air,
For in mounds of 'what ifs', lies humor so rare.
In the heights of your attic, where shadows convene,
You'll find quirky joy in what might have been.

Whispers from the Unlikely Corners

In shadows where the dust bunnies play,
The lost socks giggle, hiding away.
A plastic fork, a true sage it seems,
Whispers of laughter in forgotten dreams.

The cat's toy mouse holds tales so profound,
Of midnight adventures that never found ground.
A bustling clutter in every nook,
Revealing odd treasures, come take a look.

The Hidden Meaning in an Empty Coffee Cup

An empty cup sits, looking quite grand,
It might just hold more than we planned.
Steam of ideas once whirled in the air,
Now echoes of caffeine linger everywhere.

In each little ring from a spill on the desk,
Lives the wisdom of what we all quest.
It's not just for coffee, oh no, not at all,
But a vessel for musings at good morning's call.

Serendipity Under the Kitchen Sink

Beneath the sink, where the dish soap lies,
A meeting of sponges, oh what a surprise!
They gossip and gossip about dirty plates,
While odors of garlic play matchmaker fates.

A dust bunny's dance with a lost tea bag,
Amidst bottles labeled with every old nag.
Who knew the chaos could lead to such fun?
In the mess of the kitchen, new stories begun!

Ode to the Leftover Pizza Slice

One crusty slice, the lone survivor,
In cold box realms, it's quite the driver.
Dreams of toppings, now just a ghost,
A cheesy delight we all love most.

While others toss out, we ponder it well,
A relic of feasts, with stories to tell.
In the fridge, it waits with pride and cheer,
A reminder that treasures are often so near.

Lessons from a Broken Watch

Time stood still on that old worn face,
Ticks and tocks lost their race.
It taught me to pause, to simply be,
Even clocks can find spontaneity.

A second hand stuck, a funny sight,
Sparks ideas wrapped in delight.
Sometimes late is just on cue,
So laugh with every hour that's askew.

With each tiny gear, the truth unveiled,
In broken things, joy has prevailed.
So here's to chaos that clinks and tocks,
Life's a puzzle, wear mismatched socks.

Embrace each moment, a silly dance,
In misfit times, we find our chance.
So let your whims rule your time,
Even broken watches can chime in rhyme.

Epiphanies at the Bottom of a Bittersweet Glass

A sip of sour gave way to sweet,
In the glass, my thoughts compete.
Here at the bottom, visions squeeze,
Life's odd flavors are sure to please.

Lemonade dreams with a dash of gin,
Laughter bubbles where quirks begin.
Drink until sense turns upside down,
Find the crown in this silly town.

From tiny sips, big thoughts emerge,
Stirring my soul with a playful surge.
So toast to chaos, let spirits flow,
The weirdest truths are best in a show.

Each glass filled with an unexpected twist,
Life's happy hour is hard to miss.
So grab a drink, watch worries pass,
Clarity lives in a bittersweet glass.

Truths Disguised as Unfinished Puzzles

Pieces scattered, a quirky spree,
What fits where? Oh, woe is me!
Through the jumble, a chuckle sneaks,
In odd shapes, wisdom uniquely speaks.

Corners twisted, sides askew,
Searching hard for a breakthrough.
Life's puzzles often lack the frame,
Yet laughter finds its route to fame.

Though edges fray and colors clash,
My heart races, ready for the flash.
One piece missing, but that's okay,
For joy thrives in the disarray.

So here's to puzzles no one can solve,
In their riddles, our fancies evolve.
Let's embrace the incomplete grin,
For in the oddness, the fun begins.

The Poetry of Lost Socks

In the dryer, a dance of fate,
Socks that scatter, life feels great.
One left lurking, the other has fled,
Wearing mismatched shows off my head.

Worn with holes, yet tales to spin,
Each hue is louder where I've been.
Disconnected pairs teach me to cheer,
In the chaos, love draws near.

Both left feet in a zany scene,
Missing mates, yet I feel serene.
So let the laundromat's magic run,
In every loss, there's laughter won.

The poetry enshrined in a sole,
Odd socks unite to make me whole.
Dress me in quirks, let colors fight,
In the oddest pairs, the spirit ignites.

The Stories of Forgotten Crayons

In a box beneath the stairs,
Lived crayons with secret glares.
Red dreams of becoming a fire truck,
Blue wished to swim, oh what luck!

Green was convinced that he could climb,
While yellow expressed thoughts in rhyme.
They plotted a trip to the moon,
But then lost their heads, oh what a cartoon!

Crayons with stories, oh so grand,
Doodling adventures, hand in hand.
Though forgotten, they still had fun,
In the corner where dreams never shun.

So if you find them, give them a shout,
Their tales are funny, there's no doubt.
For who knows what colors can really do,
When the world is gray, they'll brighten your view!

Unveiling Truths in the Attic Chaos

In the attic, dust motes dance,
With boxes stacked in a haphazard prance.
A typewriter hummed a tune from the past,
While a doll's head rolled, quite unsurpassed.

Old photos sighed with forgotten smiles,
An umbrella dreamed of stormy miles.
A hat with feathers declared it was wise,
But just a squirrel made off with the prize.

Underneath layers of long-lost toys,
Resided remnants of cheeky joys.
Secrets whispered through cracked floorboards,
While mice hosted shows, ignoring our hoards.

In this madness, laughter ignites,
Every relic spins quirky delights.
So embrace the mess, no need for a map,
For buried treasures just need a slap!

Melodies from Rusty Hinges

There's music in the creaks of the door,
Rusty hinges sing tales of yore.
With every swing, a note will play,
A symphony of dust in disarray.

An old chair squeaked in rhythm divine,
As it rocked back and forth, sipping time.
Echoes of laughter, the ghosts of the past,
Clap along just to have a blast.

The window sighed as it opened wide,
Whispering secrets it dared not hide.
And in the breeze, there floated a tune,
A polka made merry by the light of the moon.

So listen close to the sounds of your home,
For even the weird has its style and its comb.
In every nook, where oddities cling,
There's a melody waiting, oh let it ring!

The Geometry of Wildflower Roads

On roads paved with wildflowers bright,
Mathematics of beauty takes flight.
Numbers and petals in curious arrays,
Adding up laughter on sunny days.

Triangles crouched under clover's embrace,
Circles of daisies danced with grace.
An equation of sunshine and sassy bees,
Calculating joy in the rustling leaves.

Parallel paths weave through the green,
Forming a tapestry, colorful and keen.
As butterflies flit, vectors align,
In the garden of whims, we sip sweet thyme.

So take a stroll on this path so weird,
Where mathematics marries the whims we've revered.
In every wild bloom, geometry's found,
A lesson in joy, so beautifully sound!

Satori at the Crosswalk

A pigeon struts with purpose clear,
Waving wings like it owns the sphere.
Crosswalk lights blink in cowardice,
While I ponder life's sweet nonsense.

A stop sign holds a secret lore,
What if it wants to be much more?
Traffic jams are just a dance,
Of fenders twirling 'neath driver's glance.

Squirrels barter acorns like stocks,
Meanwhile, I ponder paradox.
The world's a circus, loud and free,
But I'm just watching, sipping tea.

In a crosswalk where hopes collide,
I find this life feels like a ride.
A stroll through chaos, dare I?
For wisdom hides where cars comply.

The Hidden Symphony of Everyday Objects

A fork whispers to the plastic spoon,
"We both slice through this charming tune."
The kettle hums a jazzy beat,
While socks conspire to dance on feet.

A broom shakes its bristles to the sky,
Chasing dust bunnies as they fly.
The fridge moans like an opera star,
Entranced by leftovers from afar.

A toaster chimes a melody bright,
While the clock ticks in comic fright.
The closet hides a concert grand,
It reveals magic at my command.

In every space a score awaits,
Funky sounds from mundane states.
Listen closely, and you will find,
Life's odd rhythm fuels the mind.

Conversations with the Temptation of Stagnation

A couch and I have had a chat,
It insists that I simply nap.
"Why get up? Just rest your head,
The snacks are near, the world can wait!"

The TV beckons with its shows,
Reality, my heart still bows.
"Why venture out when here's the fun?
Let's binge and dance—oh, what a run!"

The fridge delivers tempting treats,
Its siren call, a symphony sweet.
I ponder if the world outside,
Could compete with this delight inside.

Yet somewhere deep, the urge does rise,
To leap from cushions, claim the skies.
Stagnation laughs, but here's the deal,
The weird life blooms lest we conceal.

Whispers in the Forgotten Corners

In dusty shelves, I hear them breathe,
Old photos, books, their tales deceive.
Each corner holds a tale so bright,
In secret shadows, day meets night.

The dust bunny giggles at a sock,
Playfully hiding behind the clock.
A lightbulb flickers with dreams once bold,
It longs for stories left untold.

A mop dreams it's a maestro cool,
Conducting cleanliness at the school.
The vacuum offers tales of the floor,
It's whispered love, a heart to explore.

In corners where sunlight fails to pierce,
Whispers dwell where the odd ones cheer.
Listen close, and you might agree,
This life's a stage, absurd and free.

Serenade of the Quirky Compass

In a teapot, lost my way,
With spoons that sang and danced all day.
Maps of butter on a slice,
Guiding me to paradise.

A sock puppet gave me a grin,
It told me life begins with spin.
Laughing at clouds that wore pink ties,
We jumped through hoops of silly skies.

The fridge hummed with a secret tune,
Whispering dreams of a midnight moon.
Where carrots drive and peas can play,
My compass spins in a wacky way.

So here I wander, away from the norm,
In a world where oddities take form.
Let silly be my only creed,
For oddball paths plant wondrous seed.

The Secret Star in a Broken Sky

A spaghetti star fell on my head,
It wrapped around, my dreams it fed.
While meatballs twinkled, a dance they'd throw,
I traced their trails, a cosmic show.

With a twirl of sauce, a comet veered,
I laughed so hard, all worries cleared.
Past bellies of clouds, so fluffy and wide,
I soared through giggles on noodle tide.

Each star held wishes, all coated in cheese,
The cosmic laughter, it brought me to ease.
Pasta-facts danced in the sky's embrace,
Teaching me joy is a funny place.

In this bizarre dish where stardust spins,
Noodles of wisdom replace my sins.
So if the sky feels broken and dim,
Just slurp up the wonders, and laugh on a whim.

Echoes from the Abandoned Alley

In an alley where shadows blend,
Whispers from trash cans around the bend.
A raccoon strummed on a broken lute,
As I danced with echoes, oh what a hoot!

Graffiti giggles splashed on the wall,
Each splatter of colors, a mystical call.
A pizza box sang of days long past,
Memories faded but fun unsurpassed.

A stray cat jumped into the fray,
Its whisker-twitches led me astray.
Chasing echoes with each silly leap,
In every corner, secrets to keep.

Alleyway wonders, so odd yet bright,
In the heart of weirdness, I found my light.
With every jest, and every sigh,
I learned that joy wears a funny tie.

Revelations in a Parking Lot Oasis

In a lot where the shadows play,
A cactus waved in a sunny sway.
It whispered secrets of lost car keys,
A palm tree giggled, swaying with ease.

Shopping carts formed a wild parade,
Underneath the sun, they're unafraid.
A sandwich hero, wrapped so bright,
Offered wisdom beyond the bite.

As tires rolled like dancers do,
I joined the revelry, me and my shoe.
With windshield wipers playing a tune,
We boogied beneath the afternoon moon.

So next time you park, take a pause,
In the strangest spots, find laughter's cause.
Each aisle can lead to the most bizarre,
In the heart of the lot, you'll find your star.

The Dance of Shadows on the Wall

Shadows wiggle, shadows sway,
They cha-cha chase the light of day.
A cat in boots joins in the fun,
Two left feet, yet they still run.

A lamp post taps its glowing head,
As silver spoons leap from their bed.
The wall turns to a circus ring,
Where mismatched socks become the king.

A rubber chicken, quite a sight,
Has pirouetted into the night.
With giggles bubbling in the air,
The shadows dance without a care.

Each flicker tells a silly tale,
Of paper hats that sail and flail.
In every bend, there's joy to find,
In quirky things, we're all entwined.

In Search of the Golden Equation

A penguin wears a monocle,
And sings a tune, quite comical.
With pie charts dressed in polka dots,
He juggles numbers 'til he's caught.

A chicken lays an egg of gold,
While philosophers debate what's bold.
They scribble sums on flying kites,
Arguing fiercely with great delights.

The clock strikes twelve, but who could care?
For dancing piers are everywhere.
While two plus two is fluffed with cheer,
The answers are just tickles near.

So bring your hats, let's solve this mess,
With silly math we can confess.
In numbers weird, the laughter brews,
Finding joy in silly views.

Whimsical Dreams at Daybreak

A toaster pops out toast that sings,
While butterflies sprout doughnut wings.
The coffee's brewing secret stars,
And croissants dance in splendid cars.

The moon slips in with sleepy socks,
To giggle at the wrinkly clocks.
Cupcakes grant wishes, sprinkles fly,
As pancake dreams soar oh so high.

Silly whispers in the air,
With pixie dust, they fill the chair.
The sunshine grins, its beams a race,
In every cranny, find a place.

From jars of jam, sweet tales arise,
With jellyfish that act so wise.
At daybreak's light, bizarre and bright,
What joys we find, oh what a sight!

Chronicles from the Left Shoe

The left shoe tells its wildest tales,
Of walking routes down murky trails.
With laces tied in knots of glee,
It claims to dance with every flea.

It met a sock that wore a hat,
And sometimes ran away from that.
With tales of puddles, mud, and cheer,
It laughs at all who wander near.

Upon the shelf, it spins around,
To shake the dust that might be found.
"I'm off to conquer socks and more!"
It shouts, and then it hits the floor.

In every step, bizarre or bright,
There's magic lurking, pure delight.
With squeaky sounds and comical flair,
This left shoe leads a life so rare.

Revelations Beneath the Garden Gnome

Beneath the gnome, a secret lies,
A wisdom wrapped in ceramic guise.
He guards the weeds, the ants parade,
In his gaze, the lawn's charade.

The squirrels chatter, the daisies dance,
Unraveling life's curious chance.
What's lost may sprout from odd terrain,
A riddle tucked in root and grain.

The veggies giggle, poke fun at fate,
Whispering tales of a grander state.
With every shroom and ladybug glance,
In the oddest nooks, we take a chance.

So peer beneath that smiling stone,
You might just find you're not alone.
In garden beds and gnome's embrace,
Life's purpose blooms in the strangest place.

The Soliloquy of a Rusted Swing Set

Swaying slowly in the fading light,
A rusty swing dreams of youthful flight.
It creaks and groans with every push,
Longing for laughter, a joyous whoosh.

The metal gripes, its freedom slight,
Yet holds the tales of childlike delight.
Each rusted chain is a thread untold,
Weaving fables of heart and bold.

The knotted ropes, they remember the thrill,
Of midnight rides and sheer uphill.
In its decay, a wisdom unclear,
That silliness is what brings us near.

So don't you scorn the swing's soft groan,
For in its whispers, we're not alone.
In scrapes and squeaks, joy comes alive,
From memories past, we all can thrive.

Unexpected Clarity in a Cat's Purr

In the warm sun, a fuzzy ball,
Purring secrets, soft as a shawl.
With tiny paws, a universe spins,
In every purr, a tale begins.

Whiskers twitch with wisdom vast,
A moment's peace, a spell is cast.
The world outside may swirl and sway,
But in purrs, we find a way.

A swat at the dust, a flick of the tail,
In kitty's grace, there's no way to fail.
Caught in the spell of a calming hum,
Life's great questions grow quiet and numb.

So cuddle close, let worries blur,
Embrace the wisdom of the gentle purr.
For clarity hides where the fur is matted,
And curled up dreams leave us enchanted.

Hope Found in a Deflated Balloon

Bright parties fade into soft despair,
A balloon once soaring hangs in the air.
Its colors dim, but hope still clings,
To dreams that dance on delicate strings.

Once a giant, now a crumpled mess,
It rolls with a giggle, a muted caress.
In every crease and every fold,
A memory's warmth, a story retold.

Children laugh at its lack of flight,
Yet in its stillness, there's pure delight.
For dreams that drift can still inspire,
And make us soar, never tire.

So cherish the sagging, the used-up cheer,
For beauty lies close, ever near.
In the silence of what seemed out of tune,
Resilience blooms like a bright afternoon.

Reflections in a Pedestrian Puddle

A puddle gleams, a mirror bright,
I ponder ducks in waddling flight.
They quack with glee, no cares in tow,
While I just ponder, what's the flow?

A shoe, it lands, a splash so grand,
A dance begun, on water's band.
I laugh aloud, I spin and shake,
In sopping socks, my heart does quake.

The clouds above, they seem to cheer,
As raindrops fall, and I draw near.
To glimpse the world in wobbly sight,
And chase the colors, pure delight.

So here I stand, on wet display,
Reflecting thoughts that drift away.
In puddles deep, I lose my frown,
And float my dreams, upside down.

Poetry Blossoms from Empty Bottles

The bottle tipped, the cap goes pop,
Out spills a verse, a fruity drop.
With every sip, a rhythm found,
A corkscrew twist, my muse unbound.

The label sings of days gone by,
While bubbles dance beneath the sky.
I scribble notes on napkin dreams,
As laughter bursts, or so it seems.

Oh, who knew joy could taste so sweet?
With citrus rhymes that twist and meet.
The empty glass now brims with thought,
A nectar from the silliness wrought.

So raise your cup, let's drink and scheme,
For every sip ignites a meme.
As poetry blooms in bottles bright,
I toast to words that feel just right.

The Clock That Told a Different Time

A clock on the wall, quite out of place,
Ticks with a rhythm that's hard to trace.
It spins around, goes backward, too,
And tells me when to barbecue.

What is the hour? It's tea or maybe lunch?
A taco break or even a brunch?
I check the time, it's never true,
But makes each day a surprise anew.

I ponder life at two a.m.,
Do fish wear hats, or dance like them?
The minutes twist, a jolly feat,
In this strange world, I find my beat.

So here I stand, with clock in hand,
And wonder why the hours strand.
Time's just a shimmy, a silly rhyme,
I laugh along with misplaced time.

Game Boards and Forgotten Rules

A game board sprawls, dust on the edge,
With pieces stacked like life's own pledge.
What was the goal? We've lost the clue,
But rolling dice means, let's just scoot!

The horses run in zigzag line,
While I'm just here, sipping on wine.
Confusion reigns, it's all a blur,
As laughter echoes – can't stir a fur!

The rules we made, they slipped away,
With every turn, we bid them sway.
But in this chaos, smiles abound,
For joy is found, where fun is crowned.

So shuffle pieces, flip the fate,
In this wild game, we celebrate.
For lost in laughter, we take our stand,
And make our world, so weird and grand.

Harmonizing with the Incongruous Moon

A raccoon plays jazz under starry night,
While owls hoot along, what a comical sight.
The moon chuckles low, with a silvery grin,
As disco balls twirl, let the wild fun begin.

We dance with the shadows, a quirky parade,
In mismatched socks, we've all got it made.
The stars wink knowingly, as they take the stage,
With laughter and whimsy, we break every cage.

An alien watches from a nearby tree,
Taking notes on our silliness, just to agree.
In the oddest of moments, connections are found,
As we sing to the moon, with joy all around.

So next time you're lost, look up and you'll see,
In the chaos of night, you can just let it be.
The weird can be wondrous, so don't miss the fun,
Treat your heart like a stage, where laughter's begun.

The Alchemy of Broken Things

A teapot with cracks tells tales of its brew,
While spoons play the banjo, how strange but true.
Old bicycles rust turn into wild art,
As they spin tales of love from the depths of the heart.

The chair with a leg made of mismatched stuff,
Now hosts tea parties for the brave and the tough.
With laughter and stories, they sip on pure glee,
In this circus of oddities, all can agree.

A clock with no hands learns to tell time by sound,
Tick-tocking in rhythm with the laughter around.
The dust on the shelves seems to dance in delight,
As broken things flourish in the soft morning light.

So here's to the trinkets that seem out of place,
That sparkle with magic, bringing smiles to your face.
In chaos and cracks, there's beauty to find,
In the odd and the broken, our joys are entwined.

Reflections on an Ice-Covered Pond

There's a frog on skates doing pirouettes bold,
While fish in tuxedos perform moves to behold.
The ice is a stage, with a snowman in charge,
As shimmery reflections make the moment large.

The ducks wear bow ties, quacking tunes from the past,
In this frozen ballet, we are all unsurpassed.
With flurries of giggles, we waltz in a line,
As nature's own chorus makes everything fine.

A squirrel in a hat throws confetti with glee,
While polar bears shuffle to a wild symphony.
And the moon peeks down, on this frosty affair,
With a smile that whispers, "There's magic to share."

So glide on the ice, where the strange feels like home,
When unusual meets joyful, you're never alone.
Reflecting on moments, we spin and we flow,
In laughter and wonder, we all come to grow.

Footprints on an Untrodden Path

With shoes made of jelly, I stumble and glide,
Each step is a giggle, each hop is a ride.
The path is a riddle, twisting here and there,
Where squirrels hold court with their champion flair.

A sign says, "Beware of the gnomes with green hats,"
But they chuckle and wave, "We're just fancy sprats!"
With mushrooms for seats, we share stories so grand,
In this odd little haven, we all understand.

Each footprint I leave makes the wild dance alive,
As the cactus does cartwheels, determined to thrive.
A dandelion whispers, "You're doing just fine,"
In this strangeness, you'll see how the world will shine.

So wander with joy, let the weirdness unfold,
In the dance of existence, be brave and be bold.
For on paths less traveled, we gather and play,
In the quirky embrace of this wonderful day.

Navigating the Curved Roads of Curiosities

In a land where raccoons wear crowns,
And the trees have a knack for strange sounds.
I ventured forth with my mismatched shoes,
Chasing the tales that the oddball muse.

The signs point left, but I head to the right,
A talking lamp said, 'Oh, what a sight!'
With ice cream cones sprouting from old stone walls,
I danced with my shadow while the laughter calls.

An octopus played chess with a cat,
While a turtle offered me a friendly hat.
Who knew the path to the quirky delight,
Could twirl on a spindle and soar like a kite?

In this whimsical world, I trip and I glide,
On roller coasters made of jellybean pride.
Every twist and turn is a bizarre glee,
Curved roads of curiosities beckon to me.

The Lighthouse Beneath the Bridge

An old lighthouse sits under the bridge so wide,
With a cat named Whiskers, my curious guide.
He tells tales of fishes that dance and sing,
And the moon that once wore a shiny gold ring.

The waves are rumbling, a bubble parade,
While jellyfish jelly is happily made.
A snail in a sailor hat steers a small boat,
With doodles of treasure on an old, rusty note.

In rain boots, I stand, wading through foam,
With seaweed spaghetti, I'm far from home.
The lighthouse beams light on the cuddly crabs,
Who share their wild dreams while juggling their jabs.

These whimsical shores, where absurd dreams pave,
Beneath the big bridge, the oddest behave.
Each laugh resonates, like a joyous clang,
In this world of wonders, we forever hang.

Solace Amidst the Junkyard Dreams

In a yard where old cars bloom like flowers,
Rusty treasures sparkle in the waning hours.
A clock with no hands whispers tales of time,
While a spoon spins stories, quite grand and sublime.

I tiptoe through piles of forgotten delights,
Where bicycles dance on whimsical nights.
A vacuum hums lullabies, soothing and low,
As I dream of the places these odd things can go.

With a teacup for one, and a teddy for two,
I sip on my feelings, they taste like a stew.
A toaster and blender join in for the fun,
As we toast to the dreams that bring laughter and sun.

In this carnival realm of metallic laughs,
Solace is found in the junkyard's gasps.
Every scrap tells a tale in its quirky way,
Amidst the mess, I choose to play.

The Symphony of Lost Socks

In the dryer, a concert of patterns and hues,
A symphony plays with the socks as the cues.
One striped, one polka dot, all in a dance,
Making music of mismatches, given the chance.

The missing pairs argue, an offbeat refrain,
While a lone sock in the corner complains.
With notes of lost laundry hung out to dry,
They sing their existence with a jubilant sigh.

A sock puppet emerges, steals the whole show,
Telling stories of journeys wherever they go.
From under the bed to the depths of the chair,
Their adventures are wild, and they've traveled with flair.

The final crescendo, a whirl of delight,
The lost and the lonely unite for the night.
So raise up your socks, let them dance with glee,
In this symphony of oddness, we all are free.

Miracles in the Middle of Mayhem

In the chaos where we dance,
A cat in a hat takes a chance.
Spilled milk makes a perfect slide,
Joyful giggles, we can't hide.

A pancake flops with a flip,
Syrup rivers make a trip.
Laughter bubbles, wild and bright,
Mayhem sparkles, pure delight.

Noodles tangled in a race,
A spaghetti monster's embrace.
Slipping on banana peels,
Life's a circus, that's how it feels.

Confetti flies, a sudden rain,
Turning frowns to silly gain.
In the mess, we find our glee,
Who knew mayhem could be so free?

Stars Hidden in the Old Cupboard

In the cupboard, dusty and deep,
Lurks a treasure, secrets to keep.
Grandma's cookies, a cosmic treat,
Stars of flavor, can't be beat.

Mismatched socks dance with glee,
Lost in time, like a mystery.
Under old pans, who would guess,
A galaxy in tangled mess?

A wonky plate sings out loud,
While spoon trumpets gather a crowd.
Beneath the mess is a spark,
The starlight shines in the dark.

Cracks and crumbs tell tales untold,
Of adventures in the fold.
In the chaos, joy will spark,
Wonders hiding like a lark.

The Wisdom of Weathered Stones

On the path where stones do sit,
Whispers echo, just a bit.
Rocks with stories, ancient lore,
Grumpy geodes dream of more.

A pebble grins, its cheeky name,
Reminds us life's a silly game.
Each chip and crack, a tale well spun,
Of sunshine, rain, and wacky fun.

Mossy faces, wise and sage,
Leafy laughter, nature's stage.
Rolling stones with roaring cheer,
Share their wisdom, loud and clear.

In the nooks, we find delight,
Cracks that catch the morning light.
Weathered stones teach us to play,
In every odd and quirky way.

Enigmas Buried in the Library of Life

In a library thick with dust,
Books with riddles, we must trust.
A penguin plays chess on the floor,
Pages flipping, who could ask for more?

The shelf sneezes, a book takes flight,
Telling tales of dreamy night.
A giggle from a phantom cat,
Mystery in every spat.

Chapters filled with laughter's glow,
A plot twist that steals the show.
Hidden amongst the tomes so true,
Oddball wisdom stirs anew.

With each page, a quirk we find,
Curious nuggets, one of a kind.
Life's algorithms, weirdly spun,
In this library, we've just begun!

A Cup of Tea in a Mysterious Café

In a café where teapots dance,
Sipping dreams on a whimsy chance.
Sugar spoons in a waltz of cream,
I find solace in this bizarre dream.

A cat in a hat serves up the brew,
With a wink that says, "I see you too."
Laughter echoes, a delightful sound,
As muffins giggle and pastries bounce around.

A map knotted into a tangle of thyme,
Leads to treasures just one sip at a time.
Peering into mugs, I see my fate,
Crumpets confide, "Just savor, don't wait!"

As the clock melts and the cups reduce,
Time jests and teases, a comical ruse.
So here's my toast, my whimsical plea,
To the joy that brews in this oddity.

The Heartbeat of Basement Spaces

In the hush of the basement, a noise breaks through,
A lizard with rhythm, a whimsical crew.
The dust bunnies waltz in the shadows down low,
As I step on a spider, he strikes a cool pose.

Faded photos hang on the wall in despair,
Telling tales of socks lost, of a stray teddy bear.
They gossip of fungi and lamps with no light,
All laughing in silence, a curious sight.

I find an old couch, it's perfect, it woos,
With cushions of mayhem and questionable blues.
Each spring, a secret, a mystery busts,
In this cradle of chaos, I learn to trust.

So I bounce with the rhythm, embrace the delight,
In this odd little haven, everything feels right.
With every creak, every craziest pace,
I dance with old memories, in secret basement space.

Revelations Underneath the Night Sky

Under the blanket of twinkling stars,
I find confessions in the light of Mars.
A raccoon recites from Shakespeare's bold lines,
While socks dance in shadows, the moon softly shines.

The grass hums a tune with a tickle of breeze,
As fireflies twirl like they're seeking to please.
Up in the branches, a parrot won't quit,
She squawks her deep secrets, with fantastic wit.

I trip over dreams tangled with night,
Each step finds a giggle, a peculiar fright.
The world upside down, I grin at the view,
For every odd passion is something most true.

With laughter as stars, they light up the dark,
In the silliest moments I find a spark.
So under this sky, where the strange comes alive,
I scribble my tales, letting whimsy thrive.

Paintbrushes Left in the Rain

With paint-streaked hands, I wander outside,
Where umbrellas are hiding in laughter, not pride.
Colors drip down like a silly parade,
As ducks don raincoats; the rain's masquerade.

A canvas appears on the street full of glee,
With splashes of madness, it beckons me.
I twist every color, the puddles reflect,
In puddles of chaos, all odds I deflect.

Brushes abandoned, mischief's foundation,
Whisper of fun in a wet celebration.
Each stroke, a giggle, a riotous cheer,
In this drippy domain, there's nothing to fear.

So I dance with the hue, let my worries float,
In the joy of the colors, my spirit's a boat.
In the rain's warm embrace, with a cheeky delight,
I paint my own story, where oddities ignite.

A Journey with the Quiet Crickets

In the grass, the crickets sing,
Their chirps a secret offering.
They laugh at shadows passing by,
While catching dreams from the night sky.

A hop, a skip, oh what a game,
They croak and twirl, oh what a fame!
With tiny bows, they take a chance,
At midnight's wild and wacky dance.

They twinkle like the stars above,
With each odd tune, it's pure of love.
In every crevice, laughter hides,
A symphony where joy resides.

So here we go with crickets wise,
Their secrets wrapped in giggling sighs.
In oddest corners, cheer takes flight,
A journey filled with pure delight.

The Spark in a Puddle of Paint

Oh look! A puddle, colors bright,
A rainbow dream caught in bright light.
With brushes twirling in the breeze,
It gurgles stories, yes, it frees!

A canvas world of dripping hues,
Where even splatters share their views.
The spark ignites with every drip,
As creativity takes a sip.

A portal to the wacky scenes,
Where paint can whisper, laugh, and glean.
In stains and smudges, joy can dwell,
A messy wish, a magic spell.

So jump in deep, let worries fade,
In this wild art parade we wade.
With every splash, a new surprise,
The spark in puddles, it never lies!

Conversations with Twinkling Stars

Under the moon, the stars convene,
With silly whispers, oh so keen.
They chuckle 'bout the earthlings' plight,
While tossing dreams like feathered light.

One winks at me and giggles bright,
As wishes float in pure delight.
They share their woes of cosmic dust,
And laugh at things that seem unjust.

What do they see in the night below?
They tease with fables only they know.
With every twinkle, laughter flows,
In night's weird play, the joy just grows.

So gaze up high, let laughter soar,
In starry chats we're never bored.
Twinkling friends, how weird we roam,
In their gleaming light, I find my home.

Treasures Beneath the Spilled Milk

A splash! Oh no! It hit the floor,
A sea of white, oh what a lore!
But in this mess of milky cheer,
Lie treasures waiting to appear.

With cereal boats that float around,
And spoonfuls of laughter spin and pound.
Each drop a story, each swirl a song,
In this milky chaos, we all belong.

So gather round, don't walk away,
In splattered joy, let's choose to play.
A hidden kingdom, there it lies,
Where silly dreams and giggles rise.

So here's to spills as gifts to find,
In every flaw, fun's intertwined.
The mess is magic, this we see,
A treasure trove of jubilee!

Eulogies for Abandoned Parking Lots

In lots where weeds do poke and play,
Once cars would dance, now shadows sway.
Forgotten dreams in cracked tar lay,
A symphony of rust, decay.

The old sign creaks in a salty breeze,
Its letters shuffle like lost keys.
No more bustling with laughter and ease,
Just echoes of urgency, if you please.

Ghosts of drivers haunt the lanes,
Their stories draped in oil stains.
A fusion of past and present gains,
A stage where laughter softly reigns.

Yet here's to lots, with faded plans,
Where pigeons strut, in casual bands.
In every corner, life still stands,
With humor packed in parking brands.

Dreams Nestled in Yesterday's News

Oh, yesterday's paper, crinkled and worn,
In ink-stained dreams, new ideas are born.
The headlines shout, in a chorus, forlorn,
Yet in the margins, hope is still sworn.

Cereal box fortunes linger in sight,
Offering wisdom that's hilariously trite.
"Tomorrow's weather?" seems vaguely polite,
As cat memes lick at the edges of night.

The classifieds whisper of odd things to buy,
A trampoline made for squirrels to fly.
In the folds of the paper, you can't deny,
Laughter blooms where flat stories lie.

So coffee in hand, flip pages with glee,
Find joy in the trivial, wild, and free.
In yesterday's news, such fun mystery,
Weird wonders await, just for you and me.

Harmony from the Cracks in the Sidewalk

Little flowers sprout with a sly, cheeky grin,
Breaking concrete, like they're in a win.
Nature's rebellion, oh let the fun begin,
A tune of resilience, it plays within.

Sidewalks whisper strange tales of old,
Of rollerblades lost, and secrets of gold.
Each chip and crack, a story retold,
Humor in chaos, the bold and the bold.

In puddles, reflections of clouds wearing hats,
Dance in the splashes while nearby, a cat.
A chorus of laughter in this urban spat,
Where life finds rhythm, no matter where at.

So walk jauntily on these patched up tracks,
Each step reveals what the ground always lacks.
In the dance of the weird, freedom attacks,
And harmony grows from those curious cracks.

Discoveries in the Faded Pages of a Diary

Once a diary held a teenage plight,
With scribbles of crushes, dreams taking flight.
Now faded dates tell of late-night fights,
And banana peels launched at morning light.

Each entry unfolds like a clumsy ballet,
With doodles of unicorns marking the day.
Lost socks and school crushes, oh what a fray,
Life's messy confessions come out to play.

Pages worn thin share secrets with flair,
Of bubblegum dreams and spiky-haired hair.
A treasure trove where laughter's laid bare,
Amongst all the heartache, there's always a spare.

So flip through the laughter, the woes, and the whines,
In a diary's heart, humor brightly shines.
Each moment annotated by an awkward design,
Finding gems in the mess, forever aligns.

Hidden Messages in an Empty Jar

In a jar so clear, no pickles to see,
Hopes whisper softly, like bees in a tree.
Tomatoes have flown, and garlic has ghosted,
Yet in the stillness, my dreams are toasted.

A label all crumpled, it reads 'Do not fret',
As I ponder the mystery, and eye my pet.
What treasures lie hidden, what's left to explore?
Perhaps a life lesson, or just a wee snore.

With each twist of the lid, I gaze at the void,
A dance of reflections, excitement deployed.
The jar holds no tacos, no sweets to devour,
But it gives me a chuckle—a slight sense of power.

In the absence of snacks, creativity blooms,
As the oddest of thoughts zip around in my rooms.
A jar full of wonder, despite being plain,
In the silence of nothing, I'm destined to reign.

The Lessons of a Disheveled Map

An unlabeled map, crumpled with age,
Tells wild tales of journeys, yet feels like a cage.
North points to south, and east yells 'Who cares?'
As I squint at the lines, my mind climbs the stairs.

Each crease a new story, each stain—my delight,
As mountains of confusion give way to insight.
With a pen in my pocket, I venture to roam,
Through cities unknown, or just back to my home.

Riddles wrapped tight in the folds of the seat,
Where the compass spins wildly, admitting defeat.
Two paths that entwine—a choice from the heart,
Maybe pizza or tacos will play their fine part.

So I wander the paper, with laughter and glee,
As the map leads me nowhere, yet somehow I'm free.
What treasure is waiting, what mischief to plot?
A giggle, a snack, in this mess I forgot!

Harmonies in Forgotten Notes

Dusty old papers, they sit on the shelf,
With melodies hidden, like goblins themselves.
Each scribble a secret, a song to endear,
If played just right, you might dance with a deer!

With harmonicas squeaking and washboards to clang,
Out pops a tune where the cat starts to sang.
Banjos and spoons join the wild, frenzied rage,
As a choir of socks brings down the whole stage!

Tangled in laughter, the notes twist and turn,
With each bend and break comes a lesson to learn.
A serenade whispers, with flourishes bold,
In this odd little concert, let stories unfold.

So gather your friends, let the weirdness arise,
As the rhythms of nonsense open our eyes.
In forgotten old notes, the madness is sweet,
Join the tune of the quirky, tap your own feet!

The Quest for Clarity in Jigsaw Pieces

A puzzle unsolved, missing pieces galore,
Staring with wonder, who opened this door?
Sprinkled with chaos, like socks on the floor,
Each shape's a riddle—who left me the score?

With edges all rounded and colors askew,
I sit on the carpet, igniting the view.
Searching for meaning in cardboard delight,
As I sip on my soda, the cat takes a bite.

Assembling the chunks feels like herding some cats,
With shapes that just giggle and dance like the bats.
A corner that fits makes me jump in my seat,
Who knew that in chaos, I'd find such a beat?

So let's jigsaw together, dear friends of the night,
With laughter and whimsy, we'll make visions bright.
In pieces of nonsense, where clarity sways,
See the beauty in muddles, in infinite ways!

Synchronicity in the Most Mundane

A sock flies off, it lands just right,
My lost ideas gather, take flight.
The cat does a leap, a strange little dance,
As I ponder life's great, silly chance.

The toaster pops toast with a sudden zing,
Bright ideas swirl in the mixed-up spring.
I spill my tea, watch it form a face,
Life's chaos reveals its hidden grace.

My phone starts to ring from a pocket most deep,
Turns out it's a call from a friend fast asleep.
A dance of bizarre, the universe winks,
In every mishap, we find the links.

Laundry on spin tells tales of delight,
As I chase a rogue shirt that's taken to flight.
Laughing, I stumble, drop my last crumb,
In the weirdest of places, new ideas come.

A Journey through the Mismatched Chores

I scrubbed the floor while dreaming of seas,
Suddenly found, I was aiming for cheese!
Dust bunnies giggle, all ready for fun,
As I dive into chaos, the chores weigh a ton.

Dishes in stacks, like a mountain we climb,
Each plate a story, a memory in rhyme.
With every splash, a tune starts to play,
Weird breakdowns keep boredom at bay.

The vacuum sings loudly, an off-key song,
Yet among all the noise, I feel I belong.
Laundry piles tell tales, odd patterns emerge,
As I turn to the cleaning, my heart starts to surge.

A mismatched sock serves as a royal crown,
As I conquer the clutter, I twirl all around.
Thus chores become legends; oh what a thrill,
In the most jumbled tasks, we find our skill.

Meditations from the Bottom of a Well

Down in the well, with echoes to spare,
I ponder the meaning while pulling my hair.
Each drip-drop of water tells secrets untold,
In the depths of my thoughts, I feel so bold.

A frog croaks a riddle, strange wisdom seems near,
As shadows and whispers bring laughter and cheer.
With every plop, I consider the views,
Underwater reflections hide answers and clues.

Old coins at the bottom, shiny and bright,
Whisper of wishes made in the night.
I flick at the surface, watch ripples abound,
Sometimes, in stillness, strange thoughts can be found.

Laughing with darkness, I feel quite alive,
Many thoughts swirl, in this dive I thrive.
In the oddest of spots, clarity beams,
From a bottomless well, arise all my dreams.

Inspiration in a Worn-out Book Cover

A book on the shelf, with pages all bent,
Hides wisdom forgotten, its time never spent.
With every crease, a tale waits to spark,
In the corners of memory, I ignite a little mark.

Dust dances above, like thoughts on a dare,
Each word whispers softly, almost as prayer.
I hold it so gently, the spine starts to creak,
In an old, fragile cover, new stories speak.

Life written in margins, doodles abound,
A laugh at the chaos in the words all around.
Flipping through pages, all worn and wise,
The secrets of laughter flash in my eyes.

From binds that are tattered, I scour and seek,
In the simplest corners, inspiration will peek.
This quirky old book, with its tales on a shelf,
Whispers of wonder, saying, "Be just yourself!"

The Puzzles of an Unusual Library

In a library filled with gnomes,
Old books whisper tales of homes.
A cat reads dreams of milk and fish,
While a chair grants every reader's wish.

Pages flutter like a startled bird,
Pen to ink, oh, how absurd!
Stickers dance, and shelves collide,
The librarian wears a walrus hide.

Chapters twist like pretzel shapes,
While meaning jumps between the tapes.
Mysterious tomes with polka dot print,
Sighing secrets that would give you a hint.

So wander here with a smile so wide,
In a place where weirdness won't hide.
Each riddle's laughter sparks delight,
Within this library, all feels right.

Unfolding Secrets of Wet Sand Castles

On the shore, where waves blabber,
A castle built without much labor.
Turtles wear crowns made of dreams,
While the ocean plots with its streams.

Sandy towers lean to one side,
Mermaids giggle, nowhere to hide.
Each grain's a story, fun and bold,
Whispering secrets the sea has told.

A seagull steals a tiny flag,
While crabs on parade do the brag.
With each tide, the laughter spills,
In wet sand's grip, we chase our thrills.

So come and join in this sandy spree,
Where purpose hides by the salty sea.
Here, memories are crafted and spun,
In castles that vanish — oh, what fun!

The Auras of Lost Toys

In a attic, old toys come alive,
Giggling softly, they import their jive.
A bear with a top hat and shiny shoes,
Confesses missed dances and funny blues.

Marbles roll like lost little moons,
While dolls share tales of wild afternoons.
A stuffed dog takes a snooze on a shelf,
Dreaming of treasures that found their elf.

A yo-yo sings a melody sweet,
Each bounce reminds us — life can't be beat!
The echoes of laughter whirl and twirl,
In this toy kingdom, chaos does unfurl.

So peek in the corners, and take a glance,
Where cuddly secrets still love to dance.
The magic is weird, but oh so real,
In dust-covered corners, the joy we feel.

Curiosities in the Catacombs of Thought

In catacombs of tangled mind,
Ideas dart away, hard to find.
A thought hugs a shadow, giggles loud,
While doubts dance like a restless crowd.

Wisdom wears mismatched shoes,
As creativity sings the blues.
Monsters of worry sip on tea,
While grandeur hides under a leafy tree.

In darkened corners, whispers play,
Chasing moonbeams that wander astray.
A spark's a trickster, hiding well,
Creating puzzles like a magic spell.

So roam these halls, let your mind be free,
In the oddness of thought, love's a key.
Where giggles sprout, ideas will bloom,
In each cranny, bright visions loom.

The Art of Listening to a Lonely Streetlamp

In the glow of a flick'ry light,
I swear it whispers secrets bright.
A glow-worm fashion, standing tall,
With wisdom for all who dare to call.

It hums of moths and lost dog barks,
And dreams of nights with wayward sparks.
A streetlamp's chat is quite absurd,
Yet deep within, there's truth unheard.

So grab a stool and lend an ear,
To tales of folks who've passed quite near.
For in its flicker and gentle sway,
Our lives unfold in a curious way.

A dance of shadows, light and shade,
Its tales of life, they never fade.
In the quiet buzz of night's embrace,
A lonely lamp finds its space.

Introspection in the Whirl of a Fidget Spinner

Round and round, it spins with flair,
A tiny cyclone with empty air.
In the whirl, I ponder life's grand plan,
Like a dizzy bee who forgot to land.

The world a blur, thoughts take flight,
As I chase them down in silly delight.
Epiphanies flash like a neon sign,
In moments wrapped in a toylike twine.

Around it goes, a playful trance,
Reminds me to give laughter a chance.
Life's a spin, both wild and tame,
In the chaos, we're all the same.

So let it whirl, let it beam,
With every spin, I chase a dream.
Fidgeting with purpose, I discover,
Silly joys that help me recover.

Destiny Written in the Sand

On a beach where castles crumble low,
I scribble dreams that ebb and flow.
The waves erasing my shiny plans,
Yet I laugh along with the dance of sands.

A seagull cackles as I draw,
My pathways curly, a real faux pas.
But in each stroke of my wooden stick,
I chase the mysteries, quirky and thick.

Footprints trail off, then fade from sight,
As I tumble down, what a silly plight!
Life is written but washed away,
A comic script in which we play.

So here I stand, with grains in hand,
Making sense of the shifting land.
Each ripple says, 'Laugh, don't despair,'
For in this chaos, purpose is rare.

Chronicles of the Dusty Qwerty

In the twilight glow of a tired screen,
An ancient keyboard, quite obscene.
Each dusty key, a tale untold,
Of half-written dreams and jokes too bold.

Fingers dance on mystery's plane,
Typing words as if playing a game.
Caps lock on, they shout a cheer,
While space bar leaps into a leer.

The quirky clicks echo through time,
Each typo a jumbled nursery rhyme.
The history of thoughts in a typewriter hum,
Bringing laughter from the most humdrum.

So let's embrace this crazy blend,
Where nonsense and wisdom often tend.
For in the quirk of every tap,
Lives the funny truth in our writer's lap.

The Cactus and the Crystal Ball

In a pot sat a cactus, so spiky and green,
Next to a crystal ball that sparkled unseen.
They whispered and chuckled, oh what a pair,
Secrets of life both were eager to share.

The cactus proclaimed with a nod and a sway,
"Be prickly at times but don't let them stray!"
The crystal ball giggled, "Let's swirl and twirl,
Find wacky adventures, give this world a whirl!"

Together they hatched schemes quite absurd,
Predicting the movements of every last bird.
Their friendship was odd, yet it bloomed full of zest,
In a world where weirdness often feels blessed.

So if you feel lost, just look where you stand,
A cactus and crystal ball might lend you a hand.
Embrace all the quirks, let your laughter extend,
In the strangest of places, your journey transcends.

Unlikely Lessons from a Dusty Room

In a corner so quiet, dust bunnies played,
While cobwebs danced lightly in sunlight's cascade.
An old chair was creaking, sharing tales of the past,
Every nook a reminder that nothing can last.

The battered old clock ticked a rhythm so slow,
"Time keeps on sneaking," it whispered, "you know?"
From dust-covered books came a muffled 'shh,'
As if every page held a secret to dish.

With each dusty inch, wisdom wrapped in grime,
Life lessons lay hidden in the passage of time.
A forgotten old sneaker began to proclaim,
"Adventure awaits, we're not all to blame!"

So don't shy from the mess, let the laughter ensue,
In the strangest of places, discover what's true.
For every odd corner, a joke might arise,
Where even old dust bunnies can win the surprise.

Treasure Hunt in an Overgrown Garden

Among tangled thorns and daisies so spry,
A shifty old squirrel wore a crown made of pie.
The garden was wild, a chaotic charade,
Each petal a whisper, each weed a parade.

A shovel lay waiting, quite rusted and tall,
Where dreams of buried treasures would often enthrall.
Excited, we dug through the secrets of green,
Unearthing odd trinkets, what could they mean?

We found mismatched buttons, a rusty old shoe,
An ancient banana, all sticky and blue.
The squirrel held court, with its pie-laden crown,
"Finding gold isn't key, just don't wear a frown!"

So if you get lost in the thicket and plight,
Remember the garden's absurd little light.
In the curious chaos, you just might unearth,
A chuckle or two worth a treasure's true worth.

The Wisdom of Rusty Lockets

In a box full of trinkets, past treasures lay still,
A rusty old locket spoke low with goodwill.
"Open me gently," it whispered with glee,
"For inside, there's a story as quirky as me!"

It told of a dancer, in slippers too tight,
Whirling through hallways, left spinning with fright.
Yet in spite of the clumsiness, laughter did ring,
As joy often crumbles, the oddest of things.

A picture of someone with hair made of toast,
Sipped lemonade while hosting a ghost.
"Life's not a struggle but a whimsical ride,"
The locket then chuckled, "Just let go of pride!"

So if you're encumbered by worries or fears,
Seek a rusty old locket; it's wisdom with cheers.
Embrace the odd moments, let laughter ignite,
For in life's kooky canvas, everything's bright.

The Baxter's Garden of Misfit Flowers

In Baxter's yard, the daisies dance,
With crooked stems, they take a chance.
The roses grumble, feeling odd,
While sunflowers nod like a quirky god.

Tulips gossip in shades of blue,
While weeds wear hats that say, 'Howdy Doo!'
A cabbage dreams of being a star,
In this wild plot, they all raise a jar.

With gummy worms weaving in between,
They throw a party, it's quite the scene.
The carrots play chess with smiling peas,
While radishes share their secret fees.

So if you wander past this lot,
Join their jubilee, give it a shot.
For in this garden, weird thrives bold,
A bloom of laughter, worth more than gold.

Hidden Songs in an Overlooked Place

In a corner shop, the teapots sing,
Beneath the clatter, a joyful spring.
The scones are tapping, with jam in hand,
Each crumpet caught in a musical band.

A lonely sock in the laundry grime,
Hums a tune that's simply sublime.
The lint gathers, doing a jig,
While mismatched pairs form a conga gig.

The ceiling fan spins a dizzy ballet,
While old hats reminisce about their heyday.
With every glance, there's something to find,
Hidden tunes for the curious mind.

So keep your ears open, don't let them stray,
For songs are lurking in strange display.
In overlooked spots, joy's sure to bloom,
Like a rabbit hiding in a vintage room.

The Bridge Between Silence and Sound

A bridge made of noodles, twisted and wide,
Connects the whispers to laughter's tide.
Chickens in tuxedos march with flair,
Clucking a symphony, beyond compare.

Echoes leap from the riverbank trees,
Where crickets chirp sweet melodies.
The wind takes a bow, with a rustle of leaves,
As frogs offer grants for the best make-believes.

Pigeons in bowler hats scatter crumbs,
While snails with violins draw curious hums.
Every step on this wobbly path,
Is met with giggles and musical wrath.

So if you dare to cross this way,
Let laughter accompany you, come what may.
For in this realm, where nonsense astounds,
Lies the bridge where joy forever resounds.

The Clockwork of Unlikely Connections

In a cupboard once home to a lonely clock,
Springs found their friends in an old shoebox.
A button and a thimble joined in delight,
Creating stories far into the night.

Bizarre mechanisms, all clicking away,
Turning misfits into a grand cabaret.
A paperclip waltzes with lint from a sock,
As they dance cheek to cheek, tick-tock, knock-knock.

Clock hands all twirl, living life with glee,
While bolts and screws sip imaginary tea.
In this odd workshop, a bond forms anew,
As pieces forgotten find a place to view.

So don't underestimate the charm of the stray,
For from quirks and oddities, friendships may play.
In the clockwork of chaos, joy finds its role,
Weaving together the pieces of the soul.

www.ingramcontent.com/pod-product-compliance
Lightning Source LLC
Chambersburg PA
CBHW072145200426
43209CB00051B/572